I0455127

The way to exit Euro

Piotr Skindzier

9. November 2012

List of contents

Abstract

The main purpose of this work is to investigate what will be the most effective way to exit European Monetary Union (EMU) by one or group of countries. During this report we will investigate institutional way of manage that goal and it impact on market and institution of countries which are participant of European Monetary Union after the beginning of exit process. We will also try to answer the question what will be the impact of this process to other European Union members and countries which are commercial partners of European Union. As European Monetary Union is first international monetary union base on common currency but without common market and government we propose to use historical experience of existing monetary union only as example of how they work and why they end not as example of what would happen with EMU but what with high probability can happen. We also try not to present mathematical model of cost and institutional way to secure operation of this process as we believe technical details of this process will depend on political agreement between countries which will start and participate this process.

List of acronyms

ECB – European Central Bank

EU – European Union

EMU – Economic and Monetary Union of the European
Union

ESBC – European System of Central Banks

USD – United State Dollar

USA – United State of America

WAEMU – West African Economic and Monetary Union

CEMAC – Central African Monetary and Economic Union

SGP – Stability and Growth Pact

EMS – European Monetary System

ERM – European Exchange Rate Mechanism

ECU – European Currency Unit

EEC – European Economic Community

Introduction

In this report we would like to answer on main question: If there exist a possibility to exit EMU by one or group of countries? To manage this we decide to divide our essay on eight part which we decide to line in logical way to better understand the problem at first and to find must effective way to find positive answer for main problem.

In first section we would like to concentrate on historical way that lead some of the European countries to establish EMU in present institutional end economical environment. We not only present countries that decide to be a part of EMU but also try to answer the question way some of the UE members do not decide to join EMU and way other new countries on UE do not try to join EMU during past years. We hope that this will help us to better understand political and economical implication that lead countries with different economic development to join EMU. We also hope that it will help to understand way of nonuniform grow of this type monetary union. At the end of this section we would like to concentrate on countries that decide to use Euro as they currency or paged they currency stiffly or in narrow band to the Euro without joining the EMU.

In second section we would like to show other monetary union that function or functioned after Bretton Wood system fall. We will be especially concentrate here on American Dollar monetary system as it function as currency in many countries over the world without any particular institution that mange it operation outside USA. We would also try to see how Sterling Area works and what was the cause of it end. For purpose of this report we also decide to look at French Franc Zone as it use common currency and it shape and numbers of countries that participate in it change through the years. This we hope will help us to understand how can monetary an currency system function in other institutional environment than Eurozone, what are the main shortage and risk of that systems.

Section third will be devoted to manage the problem of technical way to exit EMU. Here we mean especially institutional problems to manage this process. Multilateral treaty that established EMU as currency and monetary union do not enter any legal prerequisite way to exit EMU. In this section we would like to introduce few institutional models of leaving EMU. We will try to estimate how many countries should ratify new EU multilateral treaty, how much time could take this process and than process of leaving EMU monetary institution by some country (or group of countries). We would like also to decide whether leaving EMU will be equivalent to establish national currency or if there exist way of leaving EMU without establishing national currency.

In section fourth we try to consider if there is any possibility to decide how the new optimum monetary reconfiguration create by countries that stay in EMU should change convergence criteria. In this section we will be especially interest if there exist any possibility that during the process of leaving EMU there exist possibility for EMU members to manage the Maastricht Criteria compete to the cost of all operation. This section should give us basic answer about more technical question of cost and risk that can appear during all process.

Section fifth will try to answer what preparation are necessary to manage process of leaving EMU by country that wont or will have to left by other countries of EMU and by other countries of EU. We try to discus in this section whether this preparation should be announced for public and markets how early it should be done and what could be main consequences of that preparation for all process of leaving EMU.

Section VI, VII and VIII will be devote to systematic review of consequences of all steps of process for banking system, domestic product, international contract etc. We try to investigate here how debts, prices, bones and other instrument of market could react for that process. What should be done to decries shocks that we expect to appear on different markets and in different times during process of leaving EMU.

I. Historical background

1.1. Bretton Wood crisis

First development of the common European market start fast after Second World War (WWII). In 1957 the Treaty of Rome was signet ant we can start to talk about common market between European nation in modern sens. But the real monetary integration can be placed more than decade later. In 1969 the Barre Report first introduced idea of "greater co-ordination of economic policies and monetary cooperation." This report was issued by member of European Economic Community (EEC) and was followed later by a meeting of the Heads of State or Governments in The Hague to plan the creation of "the total and irreversible fixing of parity rates and the complete liberation of movements of capital."

On August 15, 1971 after President Nixon's unilateral decision to make the dollar inconvertible to gold which cause a collapse of Bretton Wood System the widespread currency floats and devaluations set back aspirations for European countries to establish monetary union. Meanwhile, the EEC grew to include nine states.

The end of Bretton Wood system open new ways to control currency rates floating. With the EEC growing the common market could not be establish with high fluctuations of European currencies of members of common market. This lead EEC members to the decision to control the rates between the national currencies which can be see as the first step to common currency and monetary union.

1.2 1979 - 1989

In 1979 the European Monetary System (EMS) was established to link European currencies and prevent large fluctuations between their respective values. It created the European Exchange Rate Mechanism (ERM) under which the exchange rates of each member state's currency was restricted to narrow fluctuations (+/-2.25%) on either side of a reference value. This reference value was established in an aggregated basket of all the participating currencies called the European Currency Unit (ECU), which was weighted according to the size of the member state's economies.

In the late 1980s the market of each member state grew closer to its neighbours, shaping what would eventually be called the European Single Market. International trade in the Single Market could be hindered by exchange-rate risk – despite the relative stability introduced by ERM – and the increased transaction costs that this brought. The creation of a single currency for the Single Market seemed a logical solution, and thus the idea of a single currency was brought back to the life.

The European Commission of Jacques Delors passed the Single European Act in February 1986, which aimed to remove institutional and economic barriers between EEC member-states and established the goal of a common European market. In 1989, plans were drawn up to realize the EMU in three stages. Although the processes of Stage I began with the EMS in 1979, the first stage officially began in 1990, when exchange rate controls were abolished, thus freeing capital movements within the EEC.

1.3 1990 – 1994

The foal of Soviet Union lead countries of EEC to decide to accelerate their economic integration as it was seen to be answer to new problems which arise after fool of soviet block. To manage this goal the Hannover European Council asked Commission President Jacques Delors to chair an ad hoc committee of central bank governors to propose a new timetable with clear, practical and realistic steps for creating an economic and monetary union. The Delors report set a three steps plan to introduce the EMU, which will end in the creation of institutions which would become responsible for formulating and implementing monetary policy.

In effect, this transformed the EEC into the European Union. Criteria for membership in the European Union and adoption of the euro are set out by three documents. The 1st is the Maastricht Treaty of 1992, which entered to the force on 1 November 1993. Later that year, the 2nd was created by the European Council in Copenhagen and the creation of the "Copenhagen Criteria," which clarified the general goals of the Maastricht Treaty. The 3rd is the Framework contract negotiated with each accession country before joining the EU. The criteria have also been clarified by EU legislation and by decisions of the European judiciary over the years.

Signed on 7 February 1992 the Maastricht Treaty reintroduced the convergence criteria that are the criteria for EU member states to enter the third stage of EMU and adopt the Euro as their currency. There are four main criteria that have to be established to join the EMU:

1. No more than 1.5 percentage points higher than the average of the three best performing (lowest inflation) member states of the EU.

2. Government finance:

    a. The ratio of the annual government deficit to gross domestic product (GDP) must not exceed 3% at the end of the preceding fiscal year. If not, it is at least required to reach a level close to 3%. Only exceptional and temporary excesses would be granted for exceptional cases.

b. The ratio of gross government debt to GDP must not exceed 60% at the end of the preceding fiscal year. Even if the target cannot be achieved due to the specific conditions, the ratio must have sufficiently diminished and must be approaching the reference value at a satisfactory pace.

3. Applicant countries should have joined the exchange-rate mechanism (ERM II) under the European Monetary System (EMS) for two consecutive years and should not have devalued its currency during the period.

4. The nominal long-term interest rate must not be more than 2 % higher than in the three lowest inflation member states.

The 1st Stage of EMU development can be correlated to a current candidate country first meeting the Copenhagen Criteria and then joining the EU.

1.4 1994 – 1999

In 1994 the European Monetary Institute (EMI) was created under the Maastricht treaty agreement. It was created as the forerunner to the European Central Bank (ECB). It met for the first time on 12 January under its first President, Alexandre Lamfalussy. In December 1995 the name *euro* was adopted for the new currency (replacing the name *Ecu* used for the previous accounting currency), on the suggestion of then-German finance minister Theo Waigel. They also agreed on the date 1 January 1999 for its launch.

On 17 June 1997 the European Council decided in Amsterdam to adopt the Stability and Growth Pact, designed to ensure budgetary discipline after creation of the euro, and a new exchange rate mechanism (ERM II) was set up to provide stability above the euro and the national currencies of countries that hadn't yet entered the Eurozone. On 3 May 1998, at the European Council in Brussels, the 11 initial countries that would participate in the third stage from 1 January 1999 were selected. In order to participate in the new currency, member states had to meet strict criteria such as a budget deficit of less than 3% of their GDP, a debt ratio of less than 60% of GDP, low inflation, and interest rates close to the EU average. Greece failed to meet the criteria and was excluded from participating on 1 January 1999.

On 1 June 1998 the ECB succeeded the EMI. However it wouldn't take on its full powers until the euro was created on 1 January 1999. The bank's first President was Wim Duisenberg, former head of the EMI and the Dutch central bank. The conversion rates between the 11 participating national currencies and the euro were then established. The rates were determined by the Council of the European Union, based on a recommendation from the European Commission based on the market rates on 31 December 1998, so that one ECU would equal one euro. These rates were set by Council Regulation 2866/98 (EC), of 31 December 1998. They could not be set earlier, because the ECU depended on the closing exchange rate of the non-euro currencies (principally the pound sterling) that day. Due to differences in national conventions for rounding and significant digits, all conversion between the national currencies had to be carried out using the process of triangulation via the euro.

The 2nd Stage of EMU development can be correlated to a recently acceded member state entering the ERM-II, where it must stay for at least two years before adopting the euro.

1.5 1999 - 2004

On 1 January 1999 the euro was adopted in non-physical form, with the exchange rates for 11 of the then 15 member states' currencies fixed on the last day of 1998. The Exchange Rate Mechanism (ERM) was succeeded by the ERM-II, which functioned similarly to the original ERM but within the context of an extant euro currency. The ECB began enforcing a single, monetary policy with the assistance of the Central Banks of each member state, and the three-year transition period set out in Madrid began, to last until 1 January 2002. In mid-2000 the Commission announced that Greece could formally join the single currency's 3rd stage on 1 January 2001.

The euro was a virtual currency for the 12 countries of the so-called ´Eurozone´– Austria, Belgium, Finland, France, Germany, Greece, Ireland, Italy, Luxembourg, the Netherlands, Spain and Portugal. It was used in accounting, and firms could conduct euro-denominated transactions safe in the knowledge that the exchange rates among the member-states were fixed. Euro-values appeared on bank accounts next to national currencies to acclimate the populace to the new currency.

In preparation for the introduction of the euro on 1 January 2002, over 14 billion banknotes worth some €633 billion were printed, and 52 billion coins were minted using 250,000 tonnes of metal. In the run-up to 1 January 1999, the pessimists reigned, spreading fear and confusion. In the media stories mounted that such a massive currency changeover could not succeed. But such fears proved to be unfounded. Bank machines supplied the new currency the minute after midnight and citizens were spending euros within days.

The 3rd Stage of EMU development can be correlated to a member state that, having joined the ERM-II and maintaining the Convergence Criteria for at least two years, joins the Eurozone.

1.6 2004 – present

In 1 May 2004, the EU saw its biggest enlargement when Cyprus, the Czech Republic, Estonia, Hungary, Latvia, Lithuania, Malta, Poland, Slovakia and Slovenia joined the EU. This create new conditions inside EMU as new members of EU became also members of ESBC but without predictable date to be a full members of EMU. On 1 January 2007, Romania and Bulgaria became the EU members. In the same year Slovenia adopted the euro, followed in 2008 by Cyprus and Malta, by Slovakia in 2009 and by Estonia in 2011.

Today we should think about EMU as the monetary union of 27 states but with only 17 countries on 3rd Stage of integration with common currency and monetary system. Three countries – Denmark, Latvia and Lithuania are in ERM II system so we can consider them as integrated on 2nd Stage but Denmark have opt-out option to leave EMU. Seven countries – Sweden, Poland, Czech Republic, Hungary, Romania, Bulgaria – are members of EU and legally signet that they join EMU as full members but they do not introduce any plan how and when they do this, so we can consider them as members of EMU on 1st Stage. Of course there in United Kingdom (UK) which is member of EU and officially signet Maastricht Treaty but after 16 September 1992 when the British government withdraw pound sterling from ERM system after speculation attack on it value UK became only UE country that use opt-out option to not to join EMU and to not to have any legal obligation to do this.

In March 2005, the EU Council, under the pressure of France and Germany, relaxed the rules of SGP. The Ecofin agreed on a reform of the SGP. The ceilings of 3% for budget deficit and 60% for public debt were maintained, but the decision to declare a country in excessive deficit can now rely on certain parameters: the behavior of the cyclically adjusted budget, the level of debt, the duration of the slow growth period and the possibility that the deficit is related to productivity-enhancing procedures.[iii] Today only five countries of EU fulfill SGP – Denmark, Estonia, Finland, Luxembourg, Sweden – and only three of them are full EMU members.[iv] For Eurozone gross government debt to GDP is 85,5% and annual government deficit to GDP is 6%. For EU members this numbers are respectively 80,2% and 4,7%.

II. Other monetary systems

2.1 United State Dollar system

The beginning of USD system we should place in Bretton Wood on United Nations Monetary and Financial Conference, where between 1-22 July 1944, 44 allied nations signet agreement. It provide a system of fixed exchange rate with "reserve currency" American dollar. All members of the agreement where required to establish a parity of their national currencies with USD and to maintain exchange rate within ±1 % band in their foreign exchange market. At this point gold standard of currencies which was base of foreign trade and exchange rate of currencies for last 50 years was replace by USD as reserve currency which was link witch gold at the rate 35$ per ounce, so the USD was seen "as good as gold".

But the real start of the USD currency system we should place on August 15, 1971 when president Nixon unilateral decide to make USD as incontrovertible to the gold. This decision place USD ass free float currency which can be seen as modern fiduciary currency. From this time we can also think about countries which adopt USD or pegged their currencies to the USD as to joining the USD system. This process is commonly call *dollarization*. As definition of *dollarization* is in fact "use of any foreign currency by another country" we will use here this term in common meaning as use of USD by any country as their currency or by pegged their currency to USD by local law.

From 1971 many countries decide to join or withdraw from USD system. Today USD is exclusively use by: British Virgin Islands, Caribbean Netherlands, East Timor, Ecuador, El Salvador, Marshall Islands, Federated States of Micronesia, Palau, Panama, Turks and Caicos Islands and use within common currency in: Cambodia, Lebanon,

Liberia, Zimbabwe, Haiti. Many countries from this time pegged their currencies to USD from various different reason which we will not enumerate here. The main advantage of dollarization according is [V]:

- avoid of currency and balance of payments crises
- closer integration with both the global and U. S. economies
- way of fight with inflation
- strengthening of financial institutions and creating positive sentiment toward investment, both domestic and international

The main disadvantage are:

- right to issue a country's currency provides its government with seigniorage revenues, which show up as central bank profits and are transferred to the government.
- country would relinquish any possibility of having an autonomous monetary and exchange rate policy, including the use of central bank credit to provide liquidity support to its banking system in emergencies

We should also place here that the main disadvantage of dollarization of any country and their currency is problem within stability of his foreign trade and necessity to own larger reserve of dollar to protect stability of their trade or stability of pegged course of their currency to the USD.

In our opinion the main problem for countries that decide to pegged their currencies to USD is to protect their national currencies from speculative attack on it. We believe that there are no effective mechanism to protect currencies exchange-rate if that attack is plan and done correct. We can even propose that there should exist mechanism of steps that set in correct order and correct space in time always end in shortage with foreign-exchange reserve. This always impel government of country that decide to pegged their currency to USD to devaluation which in fact is living USD system.

That scenario was seen many times since 1971. We here deice to look close so cold 1997 Asian financial crisis. It start on 30 June 1997 when Thai prime minister said that he would not devaluate thai bath (Thailand stayed in USD system). This statement was reaction into speculate attack on thai bath at May 1997. Thailand government was not able to defend value of their currency and till the end of 1997 bath was devaluate by half of it value. Shortage of Thailand foreign-exchange reserve force IMF to go in to action and construct on August 1997 rescue package of 17 billion $ bailout. This help from IMF was not enough and before end of August IMF was force to construct another package 3,9 billion $ bailout. Reaction of IMF also did not stop the monetary crisis which spread to other countries of the region Indonesia, South Korea, Hong Kong, Malaysia,

Laos, Philippines. In 1997 crisis also hit People's Republic of China, Pakistan, India, Taiwan, Singapore, Brunei and Vietnam. The reaction of IMF was 100 billion $ bailout rescue programs for worst infected countries of South East Asia (Thailand, South Korea, Indonesia). This did not stop the crisis which in next years spread to other countries 1998 – Russia, 1999 – Brazil, 2000 – 2001 Turkey, Argentina. Cost of all crisis is difficult to calculate but for Indonesia, Malaysia, Philippines, Singapore, Thailand, Brunei, Burma (Myanmar), Cambodia, Laos, Vietnam, South Korea total GDP felt in 1997 – 1998 by 400 billion $[vi]. Consequences of this was collapse of many business and large unemployment especially in Indonesia and Argentina where it end in street fight and change of governments.

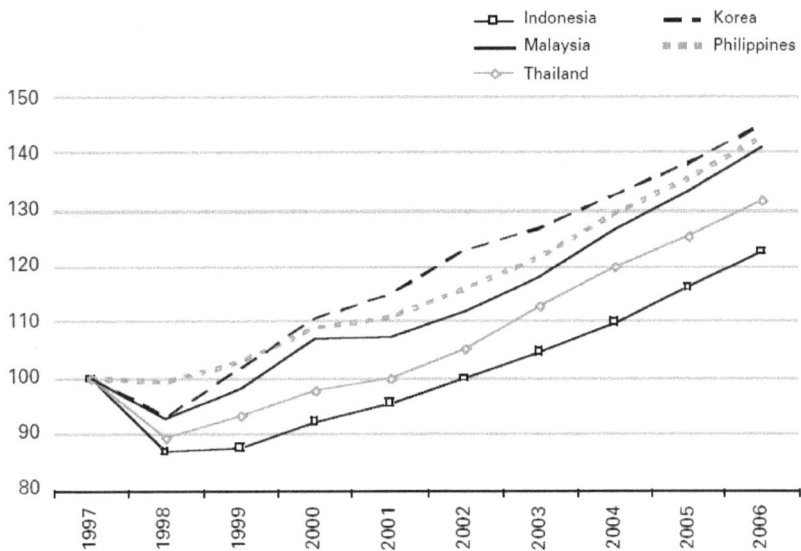

23

Change of GDP during South-East Asian crisis
denominated in national currencies

On picture above we present GDP of countries first hit by the crisis[vii]. We see that it was crisis of "V" type and that recovery was fast and permanent. We can link this to institutional reform in countries that was hit by crisis and reform of economic international organization that organize that countries (ASEAN).

From the lesson of Asian crisis we can say that weakest participant of the USD system can be easy hit by speculative attack. This attack will probably always end with withdraw of this country form monetary system, if country posses it own currency probability of that withdraw is almost certain. The crisis of trust to other country can easy spread to other participant of the monetary union as the trust of their economy and financial system is mostly base on trust that they can protect they pegged currencies from devaluations. The lack of trust will test this assumption and every country that do not past this test will have to at the end leave the system as Argentina did it at the end of crisis. The most problematic is that this scenario can not be predict by any econometric model as it start and expand not because of some macroeconomics indicator but by psychology of the markets. In that sens the crisis that was start by lack of confidence in economy of one country of USD system hit countries that was belief to be to connected with affected countries. The cost of that crisis is not always economic but also politic.

2.2 Sterling area

Before the first world war pound sterling was the most important international currency More than 60% of global trade was financed, invoiced and settled in sterling, and the largest proportion of official reserves, apart from gold, was held in sterling. Although not all the territories within the British Empire used sterling as their local currency, most of those that did not pegged their local currency at a fixed rate to sterling, as did many foreign countries outside the Empire. Following Britain's departure from the gold standard in 1931, many countries that had pegged their currencies to gold pegged their currencies to sterling instead. Group of countries that decide to do that start to be call the "sterling bloc". At the beginning of Second World War, the sterling bloc countries within the British Empire decide to protect the external value of sterling. They decide to passed the legislation in the Empire to formalizing the British sterling bloc countries into a single exchange control area.

At the end of the second world war the sterling area was the largest and most coherent currency bloc in the world, and it provided its members with full freedom of payments inside the block, but not elsewhere without a sanction of London. Members enjoyed the benefits of stable exchange rates and permanent access to the financial resources of the City of London. The British government was able to use the pooled reserves of the entire area's membership to back sterling at times when there was a US dollar shortage.

The devaluation of the pound sterling in November 1967 from £1= $2.80 to £1 = 2.40 was not welcomed in many parts of the sterling area and, unlike in the 1949 devaluation, many sterling area countries did not devalue in sympathy. This was in many respects the beginning of the end for the sterling area. The Basel agreements of 1968 were designed to minimize a flight from sterling to the US dollar within the sterling area. On 22 June 1972 Britain imposed exchange controls on the sterling area, with the exception of Ireland, the Isle of Man and the Channel Islands. At the same time Britain floated the pound sterling. The reason for this according to Chancellor of the Exchequer Anthony Barber was outflow of capital to other parts of the sterling area. Opponents argued that the real reason was related to Britain's impending entry to the EEC. One of the issues covered in negotiations for the UK to join the EEC was the problem of "sterling balances", balances held in sterling in London by governments of countries which were members of the sterling area, in many cases the result of debts incurred by Britain during the war. This was seen potentially as a threat to the stability of the pound and that this could cause turbulence for the whole of the EEC. Agreement on winding down these balances was thus a necessary part of the agreement for Britain to join the EEC, and removed the main reason for continuing the area.

After 1972 the sterling area was no longer what it used to be, but it continued to exist in that the UK still recognized the existence of the "overseas sterling area" as a distinct group of countries for the purposes of exchange control policy. In 1979, due to an improving economic situation and with the Second World War now in the past, Britain removed all its exchange controls: the sterling area had ceased to exist.

We should also stress out that the legal end of the Sterling area was in fact in our opinion preparation to join to new mechanism of currency's exchange-rate stability – ERM mechanism. This was beginning of part of EMS introduced in March 1979 by European Commission. A Parity Grid calculated on the basis of the central rates expressed in ECUs,the European unit of account, whose value was determined as a weighted average of the participating currencies, and currency fluctuations had to be contained within a margin of 2.25% on either side of the bilateral rates (with the exception of the Italian lira, which was allowed a margin of 6%). Determined intervention and loan arrangements protected the participating currencies from greater exchange rates fluctuations. In spite of United Kingdom entered the ERM in October 1990, ten years after it establishing, and was forced to exit the program on 16 September 1992 after the pound sterling came under major pressure from currency speculators. We interpret leaving the Sterling area legal control as step in preparation to monetary integration with EEC.

2.3 French Franc Zone

The CFA franc was created on 26 December 1945, along with the CFP franc. The reason for their creation was the weakness of the French franc immediately after World War II. When France ratified the Bretton Woods Agreement in December 1945, the French franc was devalued in order to set a fixed exchange rate with the US dollar. New currencies were created in the French colonies to spare them the strong devaluation, thereby facilitating exports to France.

The external value of the FCFA is determined by the monetary cooperation mechanisms between the African central banks and the French state.10 The cooperation is based on four principles contractually laid down in 1972 and 1973, namely:

1. A fixed parity between the FCFA and what was then its reference currency, the French franc (FRF)

2. The free movement of capital within the franc zone

3. The pooling of convertible currency reserves and harmonization of exchange controls: at least 65% of the two central banks' foreign currency income is required to be deposited in accounts held at the French exchequer – one for each bank. The deposits earn a market rate of interest. Gains made on fluctuations between the FRF (now EUR)

and International Monetary Fund's special drawing rights (SDRs) are credited to the African central banks, whereas losses incurred on the same cross rate are reimbursed by the French exchequer.

4.   The French exchequer guarantees convertibility of the FCFA, being obliged to exchange it for FRF (now EUR) at all times. The implication of this is that the special accounts held with the French exchequer, which function as the commercial accounts for the franc zone countries' external transactions, can be overdrawn without limit by the two African central banks if their own convertible currency reserves are inadequate.[ix]

The CFA franc was created with a fixed exchange rate versus the French franc. This exchange rate was changed only twice: in 1948 and in 1994. The 1960 and 1999 change rate were cause by changes in the currency in use in France. The relative value of the CFA franc versus the French franc / euro did not change.

Over time, the number of countries and territories using the CFA franc has changed. Some nations in West Africa chosen to adopt the CFA franc since its introduction, despite the fact that they were never French colonies.

- 1949: French Somaliland (Djibouti) leaves and begins issuing Djiboutian francs

- 1960: Guinea leaves and begins issuing Guinean francs

- 1962: Mali leaves and begins issuing Malian francs

- 1967: Réunion leaves for French franc

- 1973: Madagascar leaves (in 1972, according to another source) and begins issuing its own francs, which ran concurrently with the Malagasy ariary (1 ariary = 5 CFA francs)

- 1973: Mauritania leaves, replacing the franc with the Mauritanian ouguiya (1 ouguiya = 5 CFA francs)

- 1974: Saint-Pierre and Miquelon leaves for French franc

- 1984: Mali rejoins (1 CFA franc = 2 Malian francs)

- 1985: Equatorial Guinea joins (1 "franco" = 4 bipkwele)

- 1997: Guinea-Bissau joins (1 "franco" = 65 pesos)

In 1998, in anticipation of Economic and Monetary Union of the European Union, the Council of the European Union addressed the monetary agreements France has with the CFA Zone and Comoros and ruled that:

- The agreements are unlikely to have any material effect on the monetary and exchange rate policy of the Euro zone

- In their present forms and states of implementation, the agreements are unlikely to present any obstacle to a smooth functioning of economic and monetary union

- Nothing in the agreements can be construed as implying an obligation for the European Central Bank (ECB) or any national central bank to support the convertibility of the CFA and Comorian francs

- Modifications to the existing agreements will not lead to any obligations for the European Central or any national central bank

- The French Treasury will guarantee the free convertibility at a fixed parity between the euro and the CFA and Comorian francs

- The competent French authorities shall keep the European Commission, the European Central Bank and the Economic and Financial Committee informed about the implementation of the agreements and inform the Committee prior to changes of the parity between the euro and the CFA and Comorian francs

- Any change to the nature or scope of the agreements would require Council approval on the basis of a Commission recommendation and ECB consultation

According to this agreement we can see a Franc-zone as a part of Euro community as CFA in pegged to Euro and crucial decision for French Franc-zone will be taken in agreement with European Commission and ECB.

To fulfill the picture we should stress out that there actually exist two different currencies called CFA franc: the West African CFA franc (XOF), and the Central Africa CFA franc (XAF). They are distinguished in French by the meaning of the abbreviation CFA. These two CFA francs have the same exchange rate with the euro (1 euro = 655.957 XOF = 655.957 XAF), and they are both guaranteed by the French treasury, but the West African CFA franc cannot be used in Central African countries, and vice versa.

As we can see from history of this monetary union existing of the union do not have to be threatened by leaving of one country or by insolvency of another. Even fiscal problem of main country to which the common currency is pegged do not have to be cause of devaluation or change to another currency or basket of currencies to which CFA Franc was pegged. In our opinion main purpose for which we observe long existing of this monetary union is not economic growth, price stability etc. but better stability of macroeconomics indicators relative to other Africa countries that have their national currencies and easier access to bigger European market. This shows that existing of monetary union and cost of it leaving do not have any connection with problems that members country have inside this union. The cost of leaving monetary union can be predicted if we compare country that sustain in monetary union with country that is outside of it but is strongly link to the same markets. By this comparison we believe we can try to predict real cost of leaving monetary union especially change of GDP, inflation etc.

III. Institutional implication

In section I we mention that EMU in view of international law do not exist as a separate institution and it is part of Treaty of European Union established in Mastriht 7 February 1992. This treaty became a part of Treaty of Lisbon which create institutional background for EMU existence and only in base of this law we can start consider institutional implication of leaving EMU by on country or group of countries.

Base on Treaty on European Union Article 3 point 4: "The Union shall establish an economic and monetary union whose currency is the euro." common concurrency is establish. Detailed regulations about managing EMU can be found in Treaty on the Functioning of the European Union (TFEU) which establish ESBC and ECB in Article 127 point 2: "The Statute of the European System of Central Banks and of the European Central Bank (hereinafter referred to as "the Statute of the ESCB and of the ECB") is laid down in a Protocol annexed to the Treaties".

In the TEU Article 2 it is said: "The Union is founded on the values of respect for human dignity, freedom, democracy, equality, the rule of law and respect for human rights, including the rights of persons belonging to minorities. These values are common to the Member States in a society in which pluralism, non-discrimination, tolerance, justice, solidarity and equality between women and men prevail. " and on TFEU in Article 127 point 1 it is said: "Member States shall avoid excessive government deficits." In our opinion this two article is the only legal point which can be use by Commission or by group of member states of UE to start the procedures of withdrawal another member states from EMU without it agreement. Article 2 TEU give right to abandon country that change it domestic institution and regulations in that way that it can create treat to institutional stability of EMU system ass all – here we mean especially law changes in central bank functioning, law that allows using foreign-exchange reserve to finance deficit or law introducing institutional change in annual reporting that can create problems with transparency. Article 127 TFEU give right to abandon country that have fiscal problem and it governments are not strong enough to start and manage institutional reform which can create structural surplus that can be use to cover deficits from previous years.

In Article 50 TEU it is said: "Any Member State may decide to withdraw from the Union in accordance with its own constitutional requirements.

> 1. A Member State which decides to withdraw shall notify the European Council of its intention. In the light of the guidelines provided by the European Council, the Union shall

negotiate and conclude an agreement with that State, setting out the arrangements for its withdrawal, taking account of the framework for its future relationship with the Union. That agreement shall be negotiated in accordance with Article 218(3) of the Treaty on the Functioning of the European Union. It shall be concluded on behalf of the Union by the Council, acting by a qualified majority, after obtaining the consent of the European Parliament.

2. The Treaties shall cease to apply to the State in question from the date of entry into force of the withdrawal agreement or, failing that, two years after the notification referred to in paragraph 2, unless the European Council, in agreement with the Member State concerned, unanimously decides to extend this period.

3. For the purposes of paragraphs 2 and 3, the member of the European Council or of the

Council representing the withdrawing Member State shall not participate in the discussions of the European Council or Council or in decisions concerning it. A qualified majority shall be defined in accordance with Article 238(3)(b) of the Treaty on the Functioning of the European Union.

If a State which has withdrawn from the Union asks to rejoin, its request shall be subject to the procedure referred to in Article 49."

This in our opinion is the only one article that create legal possibility to a member-state to withdrawal from EMU as a part of withdrawal from the EU. We have to point here that in this legal conditions there can not be any other legal way to leave EMU as it is not separate political existence in meaning of international law and there is no other logical way of leaving part of international organization than by laving this organization fully.

As a remark we can point here that if we would like to consider only leaving EMU but without leaving EU we first have to consider change in law so that EMU can be seen as a separate legal existence. This will mean that there have to be at least change of TEU and TFEU in point that establish and give carries of right EMU institutions especially ESBC and EBC. This can be only manage by using Artilce 48 TEU: "

1. The Treaties may be amended in accordance with an ordinary revision procedure. They may also be amended in accordance with simplified revision procedures.

Ordinary revision procedure

2. The Government of any Member State, the European Parliament or the Commission may submit to the Council proposals for the amendment of the Treaties. These proposals may, inter alia, serve either to increase or to reduce the competences conferred on the Union in the Treaties. These proposals shall be submitted to the European Council by the Council and the national Parliaments shall be notified.

3. If the European Council, after consulting the European Parliament and the Commission, adopts by a simple majority a decision in favour of examining the proposed amendments, the President of the European Council shall convene a Convention composed of representatives of the national Parliaments, of the Heads of State or Government of the Member States, of the European Parliament and of the Commission. The European Central Bank shall also be consulted in the case of institutional changes in the monetary

area. The Convention shall examine the proposals for amendments and shall adopt by consensus a recommendation to a conference of representatives of the governments of the Member States as provided for in paragraph 4. The European Council may decide by a simple majority, after obtaining the consent of the European Parliament, not to convene a Convention should this not be justified by the extent of the proposed amendments. In the latter case, the European Council shall define the terms of reference for a conference of representatives of the governments of the Member States.

4. A conference of representatives of the governments of the Member States shall be convened by the President of the Council for the purpose of determining by common accord the amendments to be made to the Treaties. The amendments shall enter into force after being ratified by all the Member States in accordance with their respective constitutional requirements.

5. If, two years after the signature of a treaty amending the Treaties, four fifths of the Member States have ratified it and one or more Member States have encountered difficulties in proceeding with ratification, the matter shall be referred to the European Council.

Simplified revision procedures

6. The Government of any Member State, the European Parliament or the Commission may submit to the European Council proposals for revising all or part of the provisions of Part Three of the Treaty on the Functioning of the European Union relating to the internal policies and action of the Union. The European Council may adopt a decision amending all or part of the provisions of Part Three of the Treaty on the Functioning of the European Union. The European Council shall act by unanimity after consulting the European Parliament and the Commission, and the European Central Bank in the case of institutional changes in the monetary area. That decision shall not enter into force until it is approved by the Member States in accordance with their respective constitutional requirements.

The decision referred to in the second subparagraph shall not increase the competences conferred on the Union in the Treaties.

7. Where the Treaty on the Functioning of the European Union or Title V of this Treaty provides for the Council to act by unanimity in a given area or case, the European Council may adopt a decision authorising the Council to act by a qualified majority in that area or in that case. This subparagraph shall not apply to decisions with

military implications or those in the area of defence.

Where the Treaty on the Functioning of the European Union provides for legislative acts to be adopted by the Council in accordance with a special legislative procedure, the European Council may adopt a decision allowing for the adoption of such acts in accordance with the ordinary legislative procedure.

Any initiative taken by the European Council on the basis of the first or the second subparagraph shall be notified to the national Parliaments. If a national Parliament makes known its opposition within six months of the date of such notification, the decision referred to in the first or the second subparagraph shall not be adopted. In the absence of opposition, the European Council may adopt the decision.

For the adoption of the decisions referred to in the first and second subparagraphs, the European Council shall act by unanimity after obtaining the consent of the European Parliament, which shall be given by a majority of its component members. "

By using this article member-state can use simplified procedure to change treaties that it can allow withdrawal form EMU institutions without leaving EU.

Here we have to mention that we do not believe that in present legal conditions there exist way to abandon any member-state of EMU by other participants of this system without it minimal cooperation. In present conditions we can say that there exist only technical ways to restrict membership of EU country. Article 7 point 2 and 3 TEU give Commission right to suspend certain of right of member-state if it breach value refereed in Article 2 TEU. In our opinion this give legal possibility to suspend a member-state from participate in any EU institution that are mention in TEU and TFEU especially ECB or ESBC.

Summaries this section. Institutional implication of withdrawal member-state from EMU are not crucial problem of all process. If the member-state of Eurozone decide to leave it will have legal background to start and manage this procedure. The main institutional problem in leaving EMU will be that in present state leaving Euro is equivalent with leaving EU. This can be main problem with starting this process as all procedure of leaving EMU could be for member-state desired and total cost-effective for EMU as all but process of leaving EU could bring opposite result for EU and especially for country that should leave Eurozone. This can create problem of institutional imbalance between countries and institutions of Eurozone for which leaving one of members will be desirable and EU country and institutions for which leaving the same country could be economical and political unacceptable – that situation could paralyze functioning Eurozone and EU. We have to mention also that there are no legal background for Eurozone member-states to abandon one of it member. There can only exist some kind of technical ways to restrict membership of one country of Eurozone by other members. To fulfill this legal gap in EU law there should be done changes in existing TEU and TFEU Treaty. This process can be done using simplified procedure of treaty changes. In further part of this article we will not propose changes in EU Treaties as we believe this is mainly political problem and decision will be made by politics not by economist. We also are beware that starting procedure of leaving EMU from changing of existing law could stop or collapse process at the beginning as to change EMU law have to be "approved by the Member States in accordance with their respective constitutional requirements" of all EU members not only Eurozone countries. In our opinion possibility that process of leaving EMU by on of it members will collapse because veto of one of EU members is almost certain as this changes would have to create some kind stresses on bond markets which costs non-Eurozone members want be willing to pay.

IV. The optimum monetary reconfiguration

Investigating ways of exit EMU we have to look once again on problem of optimum monetary (currency) area. After leaving one or group of country the Eurozone currency area will by definition change and so there appear problem of it optimal reconfiguration. First problem of optimum currency areas was considered by Robert A. Mundell in 1961 as he point out the "unemployment can be prevented in both countries, but only at the expense of inflation; or, inflation can be restrained in both countries but at the expense of unemployment". In TFEU ECB is obligate by law to "maintain price stability " only as a second goal "shall support the general economic policies " this implies that Eurozone by definition will have to manage with problem of high unemployment in part of countries and deflation in other. As the Eurozone is group of countries with rather different industries and services from country to country there should be different fiscal policy in this countries so they can imbalance inequalities that appear by introduced common monetary policy. The common fiscal policy that is introduced inside Eurozone and in smaller part inside EU can not effectively manage with unemployment if mobility of the labour inside Eurozone won't be higher. We can observe that the labour mobility inside Eurozone have it maximum. If there exist high unemployment in one country of common currency area and inflation pressure in other mobility of employee or labour between this countries can balance that stresses. Still there are and will be a limit of this mobility. This wont be cause by legal limitations but rather by cultural and economical problems that employee have to manage to change place or type of it work. This limitation can be manage by Common Regional Policy. We believe that in Internal Market Policy Eurozone and EU manage everything what it can and there is nothing more to do.

This still left question of optimum currency area after leaving EMU by on of it member-state without answer. In our opinion the common currency can be seen in two main aspects.

First of all countries can be seen as a good members of the ares if they international trade is mainly concentrate on trade with other member-state of the momentary union. In that sense the union is profitable for every participant as cost of exchange rate fluctuation are not present and money that previously was use to protect exchange rate risk can be use in more profitable way in economy. If we observe that one of the member of monetary union start to separate from the union in trade that should be first sign that common currency area is not optimum. Outer deficits of country which use common currency can be in that situation spread to other participant of the union and cause stability problem for all the union as other countries could not have instrument to balance that type of deficits. Of course outer surplus trade of one country of the union can also create problems inside the union as it can create inflation pressure inside all the countries of the union. Common monetary policy which main goal is to fight with inflation could in this conditions cause in other participant of the common currency area depression.

Second of all as we mention that TFEU constitute main goal of ECB is to fight with inflation. This situation create for less competition countries of Eurozone potential problem with unemployment. To manage that situation that countries could decide to use Common Regional Policy to create workplaces in more competitive part of it economy. With expansion of EU in 2004 and 2007 balance of this common EU found was displaced from less competitive countries of Eurozone to new members of EU that are not member-state of EMU. To fill this gap and secure labour market from collapse member-state of EMU could decide to do:

- structural reform – to reduce cost of work and create better macroeconomic situation for business

- educational reform – to prepare in medium term condition for better mobility of the employees to find job in other countries of Eurozone

- increase deficit – in short term to protect the labour market from uncontrolled tightening

This tree way to fight with problems on unemployment inside country that are participant of common currency area should in our opinion be sufficient in medium term to optimize the currency area. We see here main problem for governments of the Eurozone that have to mange problem of high unemployment. The fastest way to do this was to increase deficit. Cost of maintain that deficit was low as long as they do not increase above value secure for public finance. When markets decide that that value have been reached they stop to borrow money for this country as EMU do not protect member-state from insolvency. The risk of national bonds was and will be different inside the Eurozone as long as there will exist national bonds for every member-state of the EMU. Since national bonds are denominate in common currency the risk of insolvency and cost of this can be transferred from one country to another by common currency. This could potentially create problem for monetary union. Bonds denominate in Euro are use as foreign-exchange reserve and if markets decide to change wallet of this reserve from one country to another this will create nominal imbalances in trade between countries inside currency area. The result of this imbalance in our opinion will be similar to what we present above as a problem with international trade outside the monetary union.

To summarize problem of optimum currency area we have to stress that in our opinion there should be system of mechanism that will regulate that area from imbalances.

We propose that maximum number of countries that are participant of common currency are should be chosen that:

- the international trade of countries inside the monetary union should be mainly between countries of common currency (or is account in common currency)

- Common Regional Policy should have enough found to help member-state of monetary union to finance structural and educational reform that help to create more competitive labour market or increase labour mobility

- there should exist maximum value of national debt for member-state – after exceed this value there should be start automatic procedure of decreasing deficit of the country; the country with to high debt should be obligate to have budget surplus in few next years

- fight with inflation shouldn't be only goal for central bank of common currency area as it potentially could create depression in group of countries inside monetary union and deflation in other part. Processes of this type could be transfer by common currency and start liquidity trap in another part of currency area which could spread by common market to all monetary union – to manage this problem we propose to resin from nominal goal of inflation present by ECB. In our opinion the inflation goal of ECB for next year should be determined as average from inflation of three countries of Eurozone with lowest inflation but only if it is above 1%.

In our opinion this condition create optimum currency area. Countries which decide to join that union should be obligate to manage that conditions. In further part of this article we try to investigate how in existing legal conditions that optimum currency area could be introduced by exiting monetary union by one or group of countries or by isolation of country that could create problem of stability for union as all.

V. Approach to transition

We try to present tree base scenarios of leaving EMU system. As we present above the EMU institutional base include not only Eurozone member-states but all EU members. That basic observation show that every model which assume renegotiation of existing EU treaty or signing new treaty can be considered as wish model. We can not have any confidence that models which require legal or institutional change in EU institution can be ever implement in propose form. We would like to stress this once more. For 10 member-states of EU that are not members of Eurozone there are no interest to change existing treaty that establish EU and also is legal background for existing common currency – Euro. Attempt of some Eurozone countries to sign new treaty outside EU that will try to manage problem of leaving EMU by one of it members in our opinion will in legal form establish new monetary union outside EU institution and in fact will create more legal and technical problem then state in which one of Eurozone country which try to leave Euro without any official regulation of this process.

For reason that we stress above in further part of this chapter we propose only ways of leaving Eurozone and Euro as a currency base on existing UE regulations. We believe that at the end of this process country members state that leave Euro will be able to establish stable national currency.

For all scenarios that we present base will be Treaty on European Union Article 50: "

4. Any Member State may decide to withdraw from the Union in accordance with its own constitutional requirements.

5. A Member State which decides to withdraw shall notify the European Council of its intention. In the light of the guidelines provided by the European Council, the Union shall negotiate and conclude an agreement with that State, setting out the arrangements for its withdrawal, taking account of the framework for its future relationship with the Union. That agreement shall be negotiated in accordance with Article 218(3) of the Treaty on the Functioning of the European Union. It shall be concluded on behalf of the Union by the Council, acting by a qualified majority, after obtaining the consent of the European Parliament.

6. The Treaties shall cease to apply to the State in question from the

date of entry into force of the withdrawal agreement or, failing that, two years after the notification referred to in paragraph 2, unless the European Council, in agreement with the Member State concerned, unanimously decides to extend this period.

7. For the purposes of paragraphs 2 and 3, the member of the European Council or of the Council representing the withdrawing Member State shall not participate in the discussions of the European Council or Council or in decisions concerning it. A qualified majority shall be defined in accordance with Article 238(3)(b) of the Treaty on the Functioning of the European Union.

8. If a State which has withdrawn from the Union asks to rejoin, its request shall be subject to the procedure referred to in Article 49."

We see this article is only legal background that give any chance to manage full process of leaving EMU without changing existing UE regulations.

We have to mention in this place that in this legal condition leaving EMU will mean leaving EU as well. We should also mention that point 2 of article 50 leave possibility to establish new relationship of leaving country with EU especially calendar of reintegration with EU that satisfy Article 49 of Treaty on European Union.

We have to mention also that article 50 of TEU can not be consider as base point from which leaving EMU will start. In our opinion there exist cases in which there is necessity to take a initial process that will prepare EU and/or member-states to use article 50 to begin legal process of withdrawal.

3.1 Member withdrawal

In this scenario nation which decide to leave Eurozone and establish national currency use Article 50 TEU. According to this article government of this state inform Commission that it decide to leave EMU and EU respectively. This is first legal step that in our opinion should begin procedure of withdrawal. From this moment there are 2 years to legal exit from EMU and EU. In our opinion it do not mean and can not mean that in this time nation that exit union should establish national currency. We propose that legal time of leaving EU should be consider as a preparation to introduction national currency. During this time Government, National Central Bank, Commission, President of ECB and Governing Council of ECB should do what fallow:

- prepare withdrawal of subscribed capital in ECB
- create stability found for country that withdrawal
- prepare if it necessary proposition of exchange-rate between Euro and new national currency
- according to Article 50 point 5 State should negotiate and ratify treaty of it relationship with EU and Eurozone
- prepare if it necessary plan of introduction national currency after withdrawal from EU and EMU and co-ordinate it with ECB and Commission

This steps in our opinion are necessary as State that decide to withdrawal could have problem to find on market funds to finance debt and deficit. For this purpose we propose to create stability found in value that should not be known for market. We propose at the beginning that value of this found should not be less than one year loan need of State. In our opinion there are legal contradictions that do not allow at this beginning stage to manage the found by ECB, Commission or other member-state as TEU do not allow that situation. In our opinion that found should be create as fast as possible and until in legal sens State do not leave EU it should be manage by International Monetary Found (IMF). Preparation to withdrawal of subscribed capital from ECB should be use to investigate what more than that capital should be transferred to NCB of State as during time of withdrawal State still be participant of EMU and will have legal right to part of the rent from Euro emission. In this step there should be decide how much of Euro should be transferred to NCB to prepare it foreign-exchange reserve for managing international trade and do this transfer should be done only in Euro or is there necessity of recapitalization NCB in other currencies from ECB reserve so that Stat could keep monetary stability. Preparation of withdrawal should also contain new agreement between State and Commission that will organize relation between State and EMU. In this step of preparation to withdrawal we propose to organize that relation similar as it was done in 1999 between EU and countries of Franc-zone. In our opinion this model is tested and give confidence that it can work in this situation – in this point we propose that managing of settlement should be in authority of ECB.

After two years we have situation in which State are legal out of EMU and EU but with Euro as a currency. In this state we propose to start another step of withdrawal. In our opinion it should look mirror-like process of introducing Euro between 1999 – 2002. At the beginning State in agreement with Commission should announce introduction new national currency and propose it fix exchange-rate. After 6 moth to year that currency should be introduce as a non-physical currency on interbank market. From this time fix exchange-rate should be floated in the margin first

2,25% to 15% at the end with if it will be necessary "crawl" devalue or appreciate according to Euro. As the State is not part of EMU ECB can use it power to effectively protect this process with NCB of State. In this step existing stability found could be transferred from IMF to ECB as it could protect fiscal stability of State. During this stage national debt denominate at the beginning in Euro could start to be denominate in national currency with secure that it could be bought by ECB from stability found assets.

Third steep will be introduction of national currency in physical form and decision of conversion all debts and actives of companies and inhabitants of the State to national currency. For this step we propose to decide at the beginning when will be choose moment of conversion and what will be the mechanism of choosing exchange-rate. In our opinion exchange-rate should be choose as average course of new currency when it was in crawl-margin mechanism. The third step should be end by freely of new currency and liquidation of stability found in IMF or ECB.

At this step we have country which leave Eurozone and have national currency. From third step in our opinion State can start new negotiation about reintegration with EU.

As it was mention before only first steep have define period of time in which it have to end. Law obligate State and Commission to manage this step in two years. Time of duration for second and third step can change depend on conditions in which they have to be manage but our view is that time of their duration should be longer than two years. In our opinion time of duration for all process depend on stability at the market and political will of State, member-states of EU, Commission, IMF and ECB.

In our plan of leaving EMU we see possibility of leaving Eurozone an EU without reintroducing national currency. In that situation State will have to exist in situation comparable to Montenegro or Andorra. This in our opinion is not desired situation for Eurozone and State but witch political problem with negotiation of new status between State and EU that can be seen as only resolution. For this reason we propose that for stability found or other financial mechanisms that should stabilize process of transfer between Euro and national currency there have to be precise period of time after which that mechanisms will expire.

3.2 EMU tightening

That scenario is some variation of Section 3.1. In this scenario we see that the main problem of EMU is situation in which one of member can be seen as a toxic member of the union. In that situation sustaining this member in the union will be profitable for him but cost of that situation could be to high for monetary union as all – we thing that sustaining in that state for to long can cause collapse of the EMU as all. In our opinion that situation can take place if member-state do not fulfil regulations superposed by the union, if it economy is dependent on international trade with countries from outside the union, if it political stability is threaten – by this we especially mean if it parliament and government are not able to pass national budget for longer than two years row, or if it vote law inconsistent with EU law.

In that situation to prevent of spreading problems that are in our opinion structural in this country EMU should consider self tightening. Of course by using EU prerogative member-state which cause the problem should be inform by other member-states and Commission about they opinion. It can be done base on existing law. In our opinion that information should contain date to which other member-states will wait to restorer conditions that will guaranty stability of the union as all. If fulfilling of this condition wont be able or there will be not enough political will in State to do this EMU should start procedure of self tightening.

In our opinion in present legal condition possibility of rule out one member-state from the EMU do not exist. In this conditions we propose to use existing regulations to isolate State from the union in institutional and economical form. This in our opinion should be step that will force State to start withdrawal plan in form that we propose in Section 3.1.

By rule out we mean use of Article 7 TEU:"

1. On a reasoned proposal by one third of the Member States, by the European Parliament or by the European Commission, the Council, acting by a majority of four fifths of its members after obtaining the consent of the European Parliament, may determine that there is a clear risk of a serious breach by a Member State of the values referred to in Article 2. Before making such a determination, the Council shall hear the Member State in question and may address recommendations to it, acting in accordance with the same procedure. The Council shall regularly verify that the grounds on which such a determination was made continue to apply.

2. The European Council, acting by unanimity on a proposal by one third of the Member States or by the Commission and after obtaining the consent of the European Parliament, may determine the existence of a serious and persistent breach by a Member State of the values referred to in Article 2, after inviting the Member State in question to submit its observations.

3. Where a determination under paragraph 2 has been made, the Council, acting by a qualified majority, may decide to suspend certain of the rights deriving from the application of the Treaties to the Member State in question, including the voting rights of the representative of the

government of that Member State in the Council. In doing so, the Council shall take into account the possible consequences of such a suspension on the rights and obligations of natural and legal persons. The obligations of the Member State in question under this Treaty shall in any case continue to be binding on that State.

4. The Council, acting by a qualified majority, may decide subsequently to vary or revoke measures taken under paragraph 3 in response to changes in the situation which led to their being imposed.

5. The voting arrangements applying to the European Parliament, the European Council and the Council for the purposes of this Article are laid down in Article 354 of the Treaty on the Functioning of the European Union."

The Article 2 of TEU which in our opinion is legal base to start tightening procedure goes as follow:

"The Union is founded on the values of respect for human dignity, freedom, democracy, equality, the rule of law and respect for human rights, including the rights of persons belonging to minorities. These values are common to the Member States in a society in which pluralism, non-discrimination, tolerance, justice, solidarity and equality between women and men prevail."

Situation of self tightening should be construct that the cost of sustaining in the union by the State that is addressees of this procedure should increase with time. In this situation we can remove main reason from which all situation start – that the State take profits from staying in the union. In our opinion process of transferring the cost of that type of crisis should least as long as the State do not decide to start procedures of withdrawal from EMU in formal sens

3.3 Uncontrolled fall

In this scenario we have member-state that was hit by crisis, speculation attack or lost it macroeconomic balance from other outer reason. In that situation EMU institution in our opinion wont be able to predict that situation. We believe that cause of this situation are not deterministic so there can be any sufficient algorithm or econometric model that will show macroeconomic indicators of approaching crisis. In that situation we can only by sure that the crisis start when one of the member-state will start to have macroeconomic problem to balance it debt, budget, unemployment etc. We do not believe that economic crisis by definition can cause problem with EMU stability even if it will long far more longer then previous that hit EMU states. Our opinion is base on observation of crisis that hit both USD system and Franc-zone in that situation we can see that if there are enough will for monetary union to exist it will stay intact and ways to fight with crisis will contain other solution than rearranging monetary union. From Sterling area foll we can get lesson that if there are not will to fight with speculation attack on the monetary union it will collapse even after minor speculation attack.

We propose in this situation to change structure of all process. First of all in our opinion there exist need for stability on market. To fulfil that need we propose at first to establish stability found by ECB, IMF, Commission and member-states of the EMU. That stability found should help affect State to balance it macroeconomic situation and keep liquidity of it finance and bank system. This in our opinion will give enough time to consider if it was only speculation attack on the bank or fiscal system of the State or macroeconomic environment change to rapid for the State so that it do not have time to adopt it fiscal policy to it. If it is the first case EMU member-states should consider change of the legal rule of functioning market form which speculation attack start so that monetary and fiscal system of all EMU state should be in future stable. If that situation is cause by second case we land in scenario of EMU tightening. The EMU member-states should act in this situation in way that was present is Section 3.2.

In our opinion this three base scenario fulfil main situation in which stability of EMU could be threaten: free will of one of member-state to withdrawal, inner political and economical problem of one of the member-state, outside influence that imbalance stability of one of the member-state. Of course there can exist mixed situation where two or even three of this conditions appear together or one after the other. In our opinion in this situation the main task is to find initial reason of the problem and start scenario or mixture of propose scenarios that will mange this problem and at the end fight with the effect of the situation.

The situation in which member-state will fell that it have to withdrawal from the EMU or it will be force to do that in our opinion is extreme. As we present in this chapter there do not exist any time borders in which process of withdrawal should end and only in scenario present in Section 3.1 there is two-year period in which we can say that one of the member-state leave EMU in technical sense. To manage stability crisis inside EMU member-states EMU institutions can only try to isolate affected participant so the stability of all monetary union wont be threaten. In our opinion existing legal condition give only that possibilities.

VI. Effect on the banking system

Present in Section V mechanism of exit EMU in our opinion create conditions that should stabilize banking system of State that exit EMU and other States of EMU. In our proposition the legal withdrawal is announce two year before State legally leave the union. In that situation banks that operate in State can for two year period still be stabilize by ECB by the loan. Of course period of this loan can be different and can stabilize banking system for different period of time. In our opinion stabilize program for banking system should not be longer that five-years loans as we predict that in five years period State that withdrawal from EMU should decide to establish its own currency, rejoin EU or stay with Euro but outside Eurozone.

More interesting in our opinion is period in which State leave EMU but will not introduce national currency yet. In that situation NCB is not a emitter of currency that is use on it territory and can not be seen as lender of last resort. In that situation probability of destabilization of the banking system in the State are in our opinion to high. To prevent that situation we propose to use some variation of mechanism that stabilize Franc-zone system. In our proposition agreements between State and EU of withdrawal should contain part which will ensure that NCB will have create account in EBC. This account could be use by NCB to take loan on main refinancing rate. The value of loan that NCB could take from this account will be negotiate between NCB and ECB every year and wont be announce public. If it will be necessary Executive Board could increase that limit after informing Governing Council. That mechanism in our opinion will create situation in which NCB will have chance to gain enough money to be recognize as lender of last resort. It will also mean that NCB will have to had margin lending rate high enough to discourage banks on it territory from borrowing as there will exist maximal limit of credit that he can loan form ECB and that using that mechanism will require to find found for it financing. This mechanism will also be restricted by short period (one year) in which portfolio of liquidity can be restricted indirectly by ECB. We propose that period of existing of this mechanism could be restricted by time in which banks that operate on State do not pay off all credit loan in ECB in first period of withdrawal or by time in which State do not start process to establish national currency. In period of establishing national currency the credit line of NCB in EBC should be reduce as national currency became fully floating currency.

We see this mechanism as compatible with propose mechanism of stability found create to protect stabilize public finance. Situation in which both of this mechanism is manage by international institution and State do not have decide voice on it period of existence or amount of money that can be transferred from it to national economy protect this process from political influences. It create also other desirable condition in which Eurozone institution will still have influence on monetary politic of State that in fact is part of the Eurozone even if in jure NCB can be recognize as independent. This will protect Eurozone from situation in which using of monetary policy instrument by the State can create imbalance in payment between State and EMU member-states. Our opinion is that situation of exiting EMU by one of the State can not be seen by it as occasion to gain extra foreign-exchange reserve by cost of other Eurozone member-states. We think that propose mechanisms protect sufficiently EMU member-states from that situation and give enough protection for banking system of Eurozone and the State.

VII. Implication for domestic mortgages, economic growth etc.

In this section we would try to investigate how the process of withdrawal one of the EMU member-state will influence macroeconomic situation in the State and other Eurozone members. We are here especially interesting how it change economic growth, inflation, domestic mortgages etc. In our opinion this is basic question for microeconomics. We think that process of withdrawal will have chance to succeed if individuals will believe that this process is necessary or will give some kind of profit to individuals how are not only basic players on the market but are also a voters how will have to give political background for this process thru the responsible elections.

In the first scenario of withdrawal – present in Section 3.1 – when the process is start by the State it can be well prepare and precede by referendum. In this situation process of withdrawal in first stage when the State only legally withdraw from the EMU system can have no significance for macroeconomic of the State. In second stage if the State is net beneficiary in the EU leaving of it structure will create lack in investment. That in our opinion will cause stagnation in economy or even recession. In that situation further transition to national currency could be stop by social dissatisfaction and if it will be join with election can stop further process of transition. In our opinion this situation can be manage by internal reform of the State or by reintegration with EU which will reintroduce structural found that help growth in the State. Further process of reintroduction national currency in our opinion is irrelevant to the situation if the State is part of the EU or not. In procedures of reintroducing of national currency that was present in Section V all the historical process that lead member-states to introduce Euro will appear again especially cost of: exchange-rate difference, denominations of mortgages domestic debts, influence of exchange-rate to economic growth, reintroduce national currency, currencies exchange.

The cost of reintroducing national currency in our opinion can be split to three different type:

- technical cost of introducing new currency
- cost of reintroducing currency for the business
- cost for all economy – slowdown of international commerce

According to Deutsche Bank analyse cost of introducing Euro was 0,5 – 0,6% of GDP. In our opinion cost of reintroducing national currency will be at least the same and it will have to be manage only by the State that decide to withdrawal from the union.

According to Delloite report cost for business (especially trade) can take 0,75% of year sales and are cause mainly by changing informatics system and increase time of work cause by use of two currencies in the same period of time. In our opinion that type of cost will appear in economy mostly by increase of inflation. Firms for which all profit is comparable to about 1% of year sale will have to increase prices or fall. In our opinion that process will appear as step growth of inflation in first half of the year when physical form of new currency will be reintroduce.

According to National Bank of Poland (NBP) report profit of reintroducing the Euro for Poland will be 7,5% of GDP growth in long period and will be cause mainly by increase of export, decrease of cost of credits etc. In year periods that cost can be as high as 0,7% of GDP growth. The increase of international trade is predicted to be 9 – 11%. In our opinion that increase in introducing Euro can be seen as cost in scenario when the State decide to leave the EMU. In that situation the State should be prepare for slowdown of about 1% of it GDP in long period (10 years at least).

Adding all this effect together we predict that slowdown of GDP growth for the State that decide to withdraw from EMU will be max. 2% of GDP in first year and about 0,6-1% in next year's. This will give slowdown of economic growth for about 10 – 15% in the period of ten years. We have to ad that this will be join with increase of inflation in first period of reintroducing national currency and increase of interest rate for business. That situation in our opinion can lead to increase of unemployment.

Mortgages loan during this process could contribute to destabilization of macroeconomic situation of the State. Increase interest rate that will appear during process of reintroducing national currency will cause also increase trouble for citizen and business to pay all type of loan. Slowdown in economic situation can lead to fall of price of properties that secure the loans and will cause a problem for debtors and banks to find new secure of mortgages. In that situation we propose to give banks and debtors time to renegotiate mortgages loan before reintroducing national currency in any form (electronic or physical). In that situation mortgages loan in the State after reintroducing national currency can be seen as foreign currency mortgages loan if bank and debtor decide not to change currency of loan to national currency. This will also give chance to inform bank client about risk, possible profit or lost that could appear during the process of changing of currency.

In scenario of uncontrolled fall present in Section 3.3 the situation in our opinion will be completely different. In our opinion it will be similar to situation that was present when South-East Asia countries withdrawal from USD system (1997 Asian financial crisis) or Sterling area collapse. In that situation cost of all process can be predicted by compering cost of help found that was use by IMF and it influence on stabilization of economy of this country. As a memento we should say in this moment that IMF help ASAEN countries by 100 bln $ loan and total cost of this country crisis was 220 bln $ nominal which was 31,7% of it

GDP. In our opinion it is most likely that cost of withdrawal one of the State from the EMU in crisis conditions could have the same order of magnitude. The GDP of most affected country which will be force to withdrawal will fell sharply and by about 80% nominal (in Euro) as it was with Indonesia. If the stability package will be high enough and will be use responsibly we still have to be prepare that cast of all process will be comparable to what happen in UK after "Black Wednesday". The cost of that financial crisis and withdrawal from ERM mechanism was 3,3 bln pound. Here we have to mention that inters rate go from 10 to 15% in one day and go back to 10% next day – the cost of that instability for national economy is hard to estimate. The spending of Treasure to fight with that situation is predicted to be 25 bln pound of reserve to stabilize pound exchange-rate. We cannot say that leaving ERM and end of Sterling Area start crisis in UK as devaluation of the pound help export.

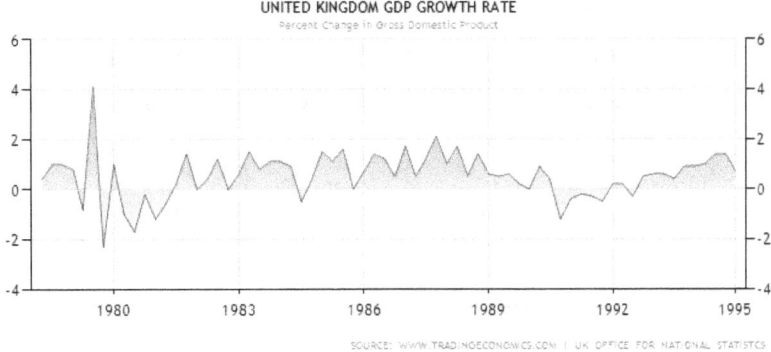

In this picture we present change in UK GDP after leaving Sterling Area and ERM mechanism

In our consideration about uncontrolled fall of the EMU member-state we have to also mention that situation of recession which appear will be complicated by the mortgages loan market which will be destabilize by foal price of properties. This in our opinion can create situation in which bank system will have problem with stability and will have to be help by NCB or by ECB. In that situation we predict that it will appear second round in which bank stop credits to the business and create another round of crisis and unemployment.

Summing this scenario and it influence on economy as all we see that situation of withdrawal during the crisis can cost GDP fall for all the Eurozone member-states of max. 30% in total (in period of 3 years plus), GDP fall of affected country that will be force to withdrawal will be max. 80% of GDP in the same period of time. Mortgage loan market collapse – compare or higher to what happen after Lehman Brother fall – and comparable problems for banking system. Recovery from that in our opinion could take decade, as it was with ASAEN countries.

Self Tightening Scenario present in Section 3.2 in our opinion is intermediate scenario in sense of it influence on the domestic mortgage, economic growth, unemployment, inflation etc. between Member Withdrawal Scenario and Uncontrolled Fall Scenario. In our opinion cost of that kind withdrawal depend on management of all process. As process will be closer to the Member Withdrawal Scenario the cost of it will decrease.

At the end we have to mention that profit from withdrawal can appear only if member-state which decide to withdraw is net payer inside the EU or it international trade is denominate mainly in other currencies then Euro. In that situation possibility of devaluations and profit of incest export that will appear in this situation could be higher then all the cost that we mention in this section. In our opinion profit from devaluation national currency to Euro after withdrawal will be comparable to cost of decrease international trade with countries that are still members of the EMU.

Summaries Member Withdrawal Scenario is the most preferable scenario if we take in to account that there could exist situation in which it can be profitable for all the participant of the withdrawal process. Uncontrolled Fall Scenario is scenario in which the State that withdraw and other member-states of EMU try to control situation to prevent Eurozone from collapse after eruption of the crisis – the lost for all the members are unavoidable and can only be reduced. Self Tightening Scenario is the case in which member-states of EMU decide to take action to prevent crisis and are ready to pay some of the cost of that action – in our opinion in this case cost are also unavoidable.

VIII. Implication for international contracts denominations

In this steep of our investigation about impact of process of withdrawal one of the member-state from EMU we will concentrate on it implications to international markets, especially international contracts denominations. We have to remind here that all the procedures of withdrawal in our model is base on process shown in Section 3.1 and processes shown in Section 3.2 and 3.3 are version of the Member Withdrawal process in which the State in first steps should be "prepare" by EMU member-states to start withdrawal in stable conditions that will give maximum chance to succeed goal of this transformation which in our opinion is to establish national currency. In that situation international contracts should be in some moment of transformation denominate to national currency or start to be seen as denominate in Euro as a foreign currency.

In our proposition problem of denomination start when the State decide to announce that they are ready to introduce national currency and show the plan of it establish. In that moment the State should inform markets about propose exchange-rate of the new currency to the Euro. This should be the moment from which markets will have chance to announce rating of loan and contracts denominate in new currency. When the State start to introduce the national currency in virtual form new contracts and bonds should be deal in national currency. That process will help denominate contracts to national currency. This process of course will be manage together with "crawl" devaluation or appreciation of new currency. That situation of course could create some nervousness on the markets but in our opinion it will be smaller shock for markets then introducing stiff exchange-rate for all the contracts and denominate it in one day. In our opinion long period of transition between moment of announce introducing new currency and it actual establishing in virtual and real sense can be seen as a advantage. If all the process will take four year plus then all the international contracts which are denominate in Euro and are shorter than four year do not have to be denominate to new currency at all as they will expire. This show that during process of introduction new currency new contract should be establish only in national currency – maybe for different markets in different time.

We can summarize that propose by us process of reintroducing national currency appear to solve problem of denomination of international debts and loans as time of the transition will create natural conditions to denominate most of the contracts to national currency. For contracts longer than five-years after full establishing national currency they could be seen as contracts denominate in foreign currency. In our opinion this will not create big problem for stability of the State and EMU if in our opinion new currency will be stable and all prose mechanisms of stabilize situation during the transition will be use properly.

IX. Summary

In this article we try to manage with problem of withdrawal one or group of member-state form European Monetary Union. In answer to that problem we propose mechanisms of exiting EMU base on existing law. With our opinion this is in present situation only scenario that create chance to start and end this process. Situation that we present in our article give also advantage of using existing institution to mange this process. We are aver of problems that this scenario could create and that we was not be able to predict all the problems that this scenarios could create but in our opinion this problems are more technical and could be manage if there will be enough time and political will to solve them.

At presented scenarios of withdrawal we decide to base our efforts in find processes that will give minimal amount of confidence to the market and societies that all the process of exiting EMU is legal and have chance to be finish in predictable future. In our opinion this give only chance that that transformation can find minimal trust in societies and markets that is necessary to manage main goal that is establishing new national currency of the State that can be stable. We also believe that this minimal confidence is necessary to do process of withdrawal without start a long period crisis.

As we mention we do not propose econometric model of that process as we believe they will be different not only because there are seventeen different countries that could decide to start that process but also that in our opinion the initial conditions from which that process could start will have basic influence for all econometric prediction. That way in our opinion we decide to propose base model present in scenario present in Section 3.1 – which can be seen as best case scenario – and variation of this base model present in Section 3.3 – which can be seen as worst case scenario. Model present in Section 3.2 in our opinion is intermediate between Member Withdrawal and Uncontrolled fall model. We decide to do that to show that base question about institutional implications (and stability), cost for economy, problems with international debts denominations etc. can be solve different in different macroeconomic situation. Still we believe that there exist base in which all models should be similar regardless of conditions in which all process will have to start. Our prediction about cost of all operation are base only on historical data that we were able to find and it similarity to consider situations.

We hope that present here point of view can be helpful and reader will be able to find some answer on question that we decide to manage in this article.

Bibliography

Commission Memorandum to the Council on the co-ordination of economic policies and monetary co operation within the Community; 12 February 1969; Barre Report

October 1970; Werner Report

Senior Nello, Susan (2009). *The European Union: Economics, Policies and History* (2nd ed.). New York: McGraw-Hill. p.250. ISBN 0077118138.

Public finances in EMU – 2011, European Commission Directorate-General for Economic and Financial Affairs, http://ec.europa.eu/economy_finance/publications/euro pean_economy/2011/pdf/ee-2011-3_en.pdf

Full Dollarization The Pros and Cons, Andrew Berg, Eduardo Borensztein, ©2000 International Monetary Fund; December 2000

Key Indicators 2001: Growth and Change in Asia and the Pacific; http://www.adb.org/Documents/Books/Key_Indicators/2 001/

Ten Years AFter: Revisiting the Asian Financial Crisis; Essays by:Jomo Kwame Sundaram, J. Soedradjad Djiwandono, Meredith Jung-En Woo, David Burton, Robert H. Wade, Ilene Grabel, Mark Weisbrot, Worapot Manupipatpong, Edited by: Bhumika Muchhala ISBN 1-933549-24-6

Britain and the Middle East: an economic history, 1945-87; Frank Brenchley; p.17; ISBN: 1870915070 9781870915076

Heiko Körner; The Franc Zone of West and Central Africa A Satellite System of European Monetary Union x Consolidated versions of the Treaty on European Union and the Treaty on the Functioning of the European Union; OFFICIAL JOURNAL C 83 OF 30.3.2010 ; http://eur-lex.europa.eu/en/treaties/index.htm

xi A theory of Optimum Currency Area; Robert A. Mundell; *The American Review, Vol. 51, No. 4 (Sep., 1961), pp. 657-665*

xii The Euro Changeover: Big Bang, Little Impact; Deutsche Bank; July 2001

xiii Deloitte (2007), Review of the Slovenian changeover to the euro. Final report – August 27, www.ec.europa.eu/economy_finance/publications/publi cation12540_en.pdf.

xiv Raport na temat pełnego uczestnictwa Rzeczypospolitej Polskiej w trzecim etapie Unii Gospodarczej i Walutowej; Zespół analityków NBP; http://www.nbp.pl/publikacje/o_euro/re.pdf

www.ingramcontent.com/pod-product-compliance
Lightning Source LLC
Chambersburg PA
CBHW072341290526
45794CB00002B/964